AF251073

SLACK WATER

Other books by Sarah Leeds Ash:

Little Things
Changeless Shore
Moment in Time

SARAH LEEDS ASH

Slack Water

THE GOLDEN QUILL PRESS
Publishers
Francestown New Hampshire

© THE GOLDEN QUILL PRESS 1977

Library of Congress Catalog Card Number 77-85210

ISBN 0-8233-0263-6

Printed in the United States of America

ACKNOWLEDGMENTS

The author wishes to acknowledge with appreciation certain publications in which some of these poems have appeared: *Bitterroot, Haverford House, The Lyric, New York Times, The Pen Woman, Pennsylvania Poetry Society: A Goodly Heritage, Pennsylvania Poetry Society Prize Poems Anthologies, Poet Lore, Poetry Society of America Golden Year Anthology, South and West, Poems by Poets: South and West Anthology, Voices, Voices International, Voices International: Surprise Party Anthology, Young Publications: Golden Harvest Anthology, Portland Oregonian.*

A few of these poems appeared in two previous volumes: *Changeless Shore* and *Moment in Time.*

CONTENTS

SLACK WATER

SLACK WATER

Consider how the turning of the tides —
like an aquatic changing of the guard —
unrolls a white-plumed echelon that rides
the beach, then is recalled. A lucent shard
is washed ashore and, as the waves retreat,
ebbs seaward; even as angers go and come
until they reach slack water where tides meet
and write a calm epithalamium.

Let all opposing people find this balance —
this hyphen-handshake on a tideless sea.
If there be darkness keep the dark in silence.
Where there is light let links of light run free;
lest all of us, defensive and alone,
be separate islands in a sea of stone.

BEFORE DAWN

It was a coastal town with sailboats on the bay.
In silhouette, a girl and boy, youthfully outré,
lingered on the sand in salty spray and wind.
And far beyond where tall masts pinned
moon and sky and a bank of cloud,
a tugboat whistle was dissonant and loud.
Back from the beach were houses set in rows
with black and white roofs like a line of dominoes.
The town seemed fictive as the legendary Oz
till the pale dawn spilled like vichyssoise.

THE ATLANTIC CITY BOARDWALK

Deep summer, and they had all assembled:
the tourists, the shop-keepers, the families,
the celebrities, the delegates, the lovers, the lonely.

Does anyone remember the old aristocracy:
nursemaids, chauffeurs, hotels, and rolling chairs;
or Broadway stars that made the lights redundant?

A quintillion ocean-waves have washed the beaches
where the Boardwalk digs its toes into the sand.
Vacationers flowed on a June tide and ebbed

with September. Only the splintered planks remain,
scuffed by a million feet that will never return;
testimony to a thousand summer loves.

Write a memoir for a lost culture;
and the Boardwalk in a salt-water-taffy childhood.

RAIN SONG

There were those autumns when we walked in rain,
snug in sou'westers. And we still recall
how one last leaf surrendered to the strain
of windy whips in fingers of the fall.
We walked on cushions of the sodden leaves
and felt a sadness for the year grown old.
We tramped on summer. Now the mind perceives
immoderate auguries of winter cold.

Time is forever. But for you and me
the seasons grow reluctant to return.
Though close by firelight now, we frequently
are vagrant rain-ghosts no one can discern,
walking in autumn. Even in our sleep
we hear the rain as lonely shadows creep.

THE GULL'S WAY

The gull's way is the windy sky
above blue waves and feathered spray.
White air-flotillas dip and fly
      the gull's way.

Their wings are sails that lean and sway
to port or starboard gliding by
to moor where sea-washed beaches lay

their satin ribbons. Gulls rely
on freedom; yet their skills display
a grace and form that dignify
      the gull's way.

SHIP MODEL BUILT BY A CONVICT

What were your thoughts as you built this clipper —
this model you dubbed the *Lady Slipper*?
In a saltier time were you a skipper?

You shaped this hull and set the sail
and rigged the halyards. Each detail
is measured meticulously to scale.

Did you think of alleys in a slum;
of a youth that was too adventuresome;
and a past that clings like chewing gum?

Was there a girl of dubious fame
in a seamy port with a foreign name,
and a room where sunlight never came?

Are towns and oceans intertwined
with memories that link and bind
a sailing ship and a tangled mind?

GARAGE SALE

A rain of sadness falls on the garage sale
this misty day in autumn
when jetsam flows from home to home

as driftwood on the ebb and flood tides.
Memories luff in the breeze.
Nothing is anchored. Treasures,

like the Flying Dutchman,
are consigned to perpetual motion;
tacking on a wind of garage sales

and finding no refuge. Only the spectral
fleet of memories returns in the night.
So we jettison our keepsakes

in a gust of expedience.
This is a day to batten hatches
on empty compartments of time.

THERE WAS THAT TIME . . .

There was that time you felt the sudden blow
of pain; the ambulance that pierced the dark,
(I pledge that *whither thou goest I will go*).
There was the lonely vigil in the stark
hospital anteroom till after dawn;
the trauma; and the unconventional prayer.
A massive door swung shut and you were gone.
And less than half of me was standing there.

Each in his hour of crisis walks alone.
The individuality of pain
is insular. Speech is an urgent phone
that rings in empty rooms . . . and rings in vain.
Impoverished morning swept across the years.
And light revealed an ambuscade of fears.

THE ABSTRACT CHRISTMAS

We witnessed Christmas from the wings that year:
Hospital beds are stark, and there you lay
devoid of ribboned packages . . . austere.
No symbols to confirm this laureate day.
The room, desensitized, was bleak as winter
after the fires of autumn wane and die.
Driven by winds of fear that shake and splinter
the mind, this heavy season hobbled by.

On casualties our personal histories turn:
One Christmas day is lost. Disaster shatters
the hallowed rituals of time. Concern
has been too much with baubles. All that matters
lies in this bed; and Christmas is abstract.
The gift of love requires no tinseled fact.

ANNIVERSARY POEM

Thus we approach the windless weather: a time
for judgments after sixteen thousand nights;
for strength against the steeper stairs to climb;
for drawing blinds after the torrent of lights.

The restlessness of youth is closeted now.
The last cadenza of winter snow has ended.
Horizons dim. But April on the bough
is tangible and green and equally splendid

by morning or in evening shades of blue.
Uncertainties have vanished. Through the bars
of jalousies the teeming avenue
blends into shadow under timeless stars.

COLLECTOR

Intent are collectors
of meaningful miscellany:

a grandfather's clock
that has ticked away the lives
of six generations of ancestors;

and Chippendale chairs
in which our forefathers
plotted the future
that we are walking through.

Old glass and china squat too primly
on the memoried shelf of time:
mute reminders of afternoon teas:
anachronisms in a blue-jeans decade.

Yellowed and brittle now, are news-clips
that provoked editorials I wistfully planned
to write; and books we read together
to the metronome of rain.

But most of all I collect intangibles:
like the music of your voice
above largo of summer waters;
and white winters
in the firelight of our love.

MAIN STREET, U.S.A.

Strolling on Main Street in a little town
you walk along all Main Streets, U.S.A.
The axis-avenue goes plunging down
to tap the nation's heart. Go back a way
to where the nineteenth century was turning
and feel the pulse-beat of the country stores.
On summer afternoons, when sun was burning
like flickering candles through the open doors,
the women swished from shop to shop, together,
whaleboned and wilted in the torrid weather.

Or if you took the trolly line, you traveled
through hyphens of green farms along the tracks
that linked a chain of villages, and raveled
behind you in a lengthening parallax.
You reached another Main Street, and well-known
pastiche of shops; the dry goods store where horse
and carriage stood; the pharmacy; the stone
bank building where financial arteries course;
the ice cream parlor with the heart-back chairs —
and bicycles with boys and girls in pairs.

Main Street inclines to science now. The buses
exhale their diesel breath on autumn haze.
But still the wrinkled river squirms and musses
the muddy shore. And still a young boy plays
with dreams, the way a small town builds its hopes.
Dusted with time, old churches stand the same
as when our fathers prayed. And on hill-slopes
they built this park with patronymic name,
and left their footprints here. We walk in these
beneath ancestral carpentry of trees.

TAPESTRY OF ROSES

Once again the sooty commuter-train
(windows half-open like leaden eyes)
clickety-clacks along the arrowy tracks
past factories, tenements, meadows;
and suddenly . . . a fall of wild roses
screens a tall embankment
in a wall of summer. No shadows,
no graffiti-brambles,
no tangled weeds, nor shambles
of winter-twigs and nettles
could quench vermilion flames. Sun settles
over like a layer of love; and red
symbols of summer spread
in a victory of roses.

FROZEN IN TIME

We speak of those summer intervals
which the selective mind freezes
in the foil of time:

The run-away pony
cutting a swath through a stranger's
cornfield, and a small girl holding fast
in her first crisis;

an old country home
where sun arrows through a filigree
of branches and tosses yellow confetti
on the shade. And deep woods
make a batik shawl to wrap the silence.

A swing waltzes in a kindergarten breeze
as though recently abandoned.
But the child is long since gone.

In the loping light of late afternoon
a schoolboy stands on a broken jetty
watching steamers cut their signature in water.
The ships still ply the river . . .

A parvenu wind
shatters the mind's excursion.
We stumble over ambiguous angers.

INTER-SEASON

The seasons turn while we sleep
soundlessly, as a leaf falls, or daylight closes,
devoid of pomp and ceremony.
Unperceived is the exact hour
when summer starts the retreat across hills
dropping leaf-shaped handkerchiefs,
as though marking the route
for a long and devious return.

We lower windows
against the sad clichés of rain
and divert our eyes
to avoid the slow desolation.
Seasonless now, we feel the caesura in time
when wind holds its breath
and verb-days of autumn
pause for a moment
on the sills of September.

HANSBERRY STREET: DEEP WINTER

Only the wind walks on Hansberry Street
this frigid day in the dead of winter,
when even the glassy glare of sun is cold.
Bristles of brown grass poke through
a shabby tarpaulin of snow;
and little mounds of sherbet-snow
dot edges of the pavement.

Rows of identical houses stand expressionless and stiff
in military alignment, right-dressed to the corner drug store;
each facade, impenetrable as a face that hides its sorrow.
Where are the people? Where are the children
who used to loiter from school,
tossing a ball or scuffing leaves in the gutter?

Layers of frost-strata surround
the frozen homes like transparent wrap;
and the sidewalk superscription of ice
is a subtle warning. Storm doors seal
a mystery of shadow — inaccessible, obscure.
Only the wind walking on stilts of time
is a Peeping Tom at the windows.

Dark comes early now — a fall of ebony snow
containing the icy interval of winter. Long
whistles of wind announce the curfew; as slowly,
one-by-one, the checkered lights appear.
And rheumatic fingers of trees
hold the moon like a thermal pillow.

BIOGRAPHY

The winter tree writes memoirs on the sky:
scrawled with old finger-boughs that tell the story
of how the wind and rain that blustered by
gave it a list to leeward. And the glory
of countless snows that crystallized the night
are here remembered by the architecture
of one bird's nest with cupola of white
(whose tenants long ago became conjecture).

How many times the leafy parasol
of autumn fell in windy avalanches,
the empty tree no longer can recall;
nor what stars swung in fretwork of its branches.
Enough to say, the tree bears its distress
apart . . . as we, our silent loneliness.

WHITE SILENCE

Is it the art or stillness of the snow
that strikes the mind with wonder? In the night
an awesome silence fell. It is as though
the trees became stalagmites, marble-white,
windless against the caverned dark of sky.
A car purrs by on cushioned catpaw tread.
And in the chambered town the sleepers lie
banking tranquility — unlimited.

The soundlessness of snow transcends the magic.
A power is manifest in quiet things:
the fall of time; dawn's drama; and the tragic
inscrutability that sorrow brings.
And stars, that turn the sky to cloisonné,
have never thundered down the Milky Way.

DÉJÀ VU

In autumn mist we wandered here before.
The same gull seemed to circle and descend.
We come as travelers to a friendly shore.

We stood here then. And now those same winds soar
above the marshes where the cattails bend.
In autumn mist we wandered here before.

We find our footprints on the pliant floor
of memory's beaches like a dividend.
We come as travelers to a friendly shore.

The mind flows back and forth as rivers pour
their ebb and flood tides. Thus we comprehend
in autumn mist we wandered here before.

When wind makes lonely echoes, we deplore
the thousand nights between that had no end.
We come as travelers to a friendly shore.

Nothing will change in ninety years or more.
Always the gull and time will interblend
in autumn mist. We wandered here before
and come as travelers to a friendly shore.

IN THE MULTICOLORED AUTUMN

They married in the multicolored autumn
and caught a ribbon of retreating sun
to bind the clouds of rain that, come November,
would drench and drain the colors, one-by-one.

Always the fall had been the saddest season:
stepchild-November, comfortless with gloom.
And moody hearthstone fires were no more warming
than summer's glow-worm in a winter room.

Then came the transmutation of the rain
from lines of metal-gray to lamé threads
of memory. Love's mortgage has been paid
with coins of sorrow. And fear's thunderheads

are sleeping now. It is as though the fountains
in all the parks of heaven rise and start
autumnal rains in soft adagio,
not to disturb the nap time of the heart.

LEAF-FALL

Leaves fall like grace-notes
with a monophonic sound;
the same as yester-autumn
on the same accustomed ground.
Walk gently, stranger;
you scuff memories around.

TREADMILL

He wakes
to wooden aspects of day:
the elemental ablutions,
the coffee and over-done toast,
the Monday-through-Friday solutions
of problems. He is part of the host
of people on subways — the ghost
of sleep on their faces.

He moves
in circular spaces
like a needle on long-playing records,
or hands on clocks of chronic time —
rounding the same twelve hours,
sounding the same tired chime.

ONCE IN CHILDHOOD . . .

In childhood he would watch the blustery sea
toss up to heaven feathers of white foam
and feel a surge of longing. Wistfully,
he wondered that the gray gull chose a home
as shelterless as sky above his head;
and fancied that the rising wreath of spray
was breath of lost adventurers who, dead,
had listened to the call he heard that day.

Now in adulthood, cautious of the wind,
he fears the attitudes of sea and sky.
Tethered to moorings, confidently pinned
to firelight stars, which he is steering by,
he listens . . . but does not detect that call
heard once in youth . . . then never caught at all.

CUP OF TIME

This inelastic moment is rigid with time.
Cajole it, pamper it, beseech it . . .
There will be no stretch nor shrinkage
at the mind's direction.

In the squalor of tenements,
where rows of cubicle-houses
nuzzle the alleys, the moment
ambles in squeaky shoes.

But the same inflexible sixty seconds
fly on pinions of love
for a young girl and boy.
All of time is in this moment.

Yesterdays are dead tomorrows;
and unborn hours hover where dim
horizons blend to earth and sky.
All we have of certainty
is in this demitasse of time.

FREE-FALL

Down come the leaves;
settling on the ground
like colored slippers
lost by a troupe of dancers
in the night.

Down come daydreams —
whirling dervishes — that spin
through the mind like leaves
in flight, to be raked away
by sleep.

TRANQUIL WATERS

Once in a silence this happened long ago.
The day is lost with the mood.
But the season returns:
That after-interval when the town
surrendered summer tourists;
and two people stood alone
wrapped in the sequined stole
the moon tossed on the water.

It is the same now as it was then:
The loud stillness when laughing voices
and ten thousand walking feet have gone.
The same deserted pier jutted far into the sea,
a causeway leading to nowhere.
All is the same . . . except for the yesterdays
that waves washed like kelp upon the sand.

Two people remember . . .
remember in shadow of night.
But the fever is over.
There is only the rhythmic roll of surf
like inescapable falling of time.

I
MORNING INTO NIGHT

Then in the morning of the year when days
were Easter-color and the nights were new
the only doubts were those that love outweighs.
The power of one and one is more than two.
Unskilled in ancient wisdom, youth engenders
assertiveness to counter and command;
as waves assail the shore and beach surrenders.
Waves toss old shells and shards upon the sand.

The knowledge of polarity discloses
opposing tides. Cool balances with warm.
In youth, time was a reverie of roses;
now winter trees link fingers in the storm.
Forever, darkness hovers over light.
Delay, delay the unconditional night!

II
EVENING OF THE YEAR

Now in the evening of the year when days
are winter-color and the dark is cold
we cling to absolutes. When nighttime stays
too long, and memories are dreams grown old,
give me your hand against incumbent fear:
that incommunicable ghost that lingers
along the shadow-land as age draws near
and designates us with deliberate fingers.

Love subsidizes sorrow. Long ago
we shared a grief; now only half discerned
in tangibles of wind and mist that blow
across the heart forever. Love has learned
intrinsic power to ride the hurricane
and read through contact lenses of the rain.

ROOMS OF TIME

Days fall and scatter
like leaves of autumn,
gone as confetti
tossed upon a bride.
Only the smiles and sorrows linger
like daguerreotypes
in shuttered rooms of time . . .
Those cluttered rooms of time . . .

PUGILIST

Winter is a boxer:
aggressive, obdurate, muscular,
with ligaments of ice
like tough tendons of trees.

When the first frost of autumn
rises from the littorals,
and wrinkles dry leaves
like hands of old ladies;
when the gray cloud over the horizon
is a piñata stuffed with snow,

we train for the bout with winter;
and summon strength against
wild punches of wind that throw
an upper-cut to windows, rocking houses,
and a jab that rattles the teeth of trees.

Resigned at last to the championship
of winter, we insulate against elemental cold
and salvage only
the long penumbra of sleep.

THE DUSK OF TIME

The winds of time blow ceaselessly.
The sands of time run out for me;
as beaches ravel to the sea
in the sweep of time.

Worn days, like sails, are stowed and furled.
A misted memory comes uncurled
in summer rains that drench the world
in the wash of time.

The thunder rumbles with new fears.
The shadow of the night appears.
But still old love ignites the years
in the dusk of time.

IDIOM OF LOVE

What can I say that others have not said:
those storied lovers, Tristram and Isolt;
all Romeos and Juliets who, dead,
still walk through annual operas and revolt
against oblivion; and Janes and Joes
whose fumbled words will never be recorded?
Our speech, implicit, coexists with those.
Our rhetoric holds memories we have hoarded.

Your voice is in locution of the waves
that daily change their moods and never cease.
You speak in silence as one star engraves
the onyx sky; and in the wind's release.
Could they have known (whose words became
    clichés)
their songs would brush our nights in paraphrase?

MAILMAN

To children, he is constant as the daybreak —
a friendly whistle on a morning street —
a man, with mystery-bag, who speaks and passes —
part of the landscape Lilliputians meet.

But to adults, he brings good news or tragic . . .
and is the binding thread — the only one —
that sews decades together, while his whistle
links immemorial mornings, sun-by-sun.

SELECTING YOUR GIFT

In this gray December monochrome,
scumbled by casual rain,
chilled by wind that is north northeast,
the stores are lighthouses
in a sea of shoppers.

A swelling current of people surges
into doorways, as water through a sea-wall,
flooding the aisles with swift confusion
around an archipelago of counters.

Not here . . .
not here, shall I select your gift . . .

On deserted beaches
where soap-suds of foam wash the sand,
and vacuums of wind are the sweepers of time,
I shall find you a conch shell,
whose walls are the colors of sunset
and whose convolutions hold the sea
and my forever-love.

EVENING MOOD

Here in this littoral silence
as the long shore dims to dark
and only the lonely wind is flowing over,

we falter in time's imbalance.
And memory, a watermark,
records the receding years that run for cover.

AFTER-IMAGE

We shall remember how the breakers hurl
their force against the bulkhead, heaving foam
in lathery clouds that feather out and curl
on wanton wind, that drives the seagull home.
We shall remember how we walked the beach
and saw the reins of moonlight draw the tide
with magic that is well beyond our reach
to comprehend. Our seashore house has died.

Never again shall we return, and yet
we feel the salty mist in random rain,
and wear the sea-moods. Who could half forget
the monologue of surf? Or who explain
how breakers roll on beaches of the mind?
Yes, we could see them clearly even though blind.

TITANS OF THE NIGHT

When afternoon retracts long rays of light
and tycoons of industry have left their layered suites
for labyrinthine highways leading home,
tall buildings do not sleep.

Stealthily, as ghosts from darkness,
comes a corps of cleaning women:
titans of the night: artless rulers of a concrete
empire, each followed by an Electrolux,
like a faithful dog-at-heel.

Concerted vacuums grind the hours.
Buckets, mops, feather dusters are tools
of domain. A thurible of detergent
fills the rooms with sanitation incense.

Companions bring a midnight snack
and exchange scanty hopes and haunting fears
in an exclusive sisterhood.

But to a walker on the blackened street
there is a cryptogram of window-lights
as though King Kong were doing a cross-word puzzle.

NEW YEAR'S EVE

The year lies dying in the cold. Tonight
our mood is somber. In this giddy haze
of cigarette smoke and reflected light
and tinkling glasses — as band music sways —
the room is listing on the sea of time.
Above cacophony that interlocks
the old and new, frivolity and crime,
tolls the philippic of the midnight clocks.

The year lies dead in winter frost. Remember
still falls the quilted silence of the snow
across those tyrannies of dark December.
And silently the nameless angers go,
as night winds die when lights of dawn appear
immaculate upon the pristine year.

DIARY OF SUMMER

Brocaded summer, like a debutante
returning from the season's final dance,
slips off her formal dress — green and bouffant —
stretches bare arms and sleeps. One more romance
has ended in the windy talk of leaves.
Once more tiara-stars seem dim and small.
Disconsolate, the painted summer grieves
and burns love letters on the flame of fall.

Then in the firelight season of the mind
we store the weathered summer of the heart;
knowing that dual tides are so designed
to give and take away . . . return . . . depart.
And even summer-love will wake, although
it sleeps in winter nightgown of the snow.

AUTUMN MOOD

Whether it be declension of the rain
or epilogue of locusts in the night
that chills the heart before the summer stain
fades from the hills, there is no way to quite
discern. So pensive is this sullen mood —
so ineludible — that you and I
assume also an autumn attitude,
knowing how soon our consummate seasons die.

Something of us goes down with summer's ashes.
Something of us rejects the fallen leaf.
A part of us is lost when autumn splashes
a quilt of color on the season's grief.
And, like the lonely cricket in dry grasses,
we sing our temporal songs while summer passes.

DEPTH OF SHADOW

Hear how the decibels of laughter break
in convex patterns pushing into air,
as wind disturbs the surface of a lake.
And see how water scintillates in glare
of liquid sunlight jarred to nervous motion.
Or, like the agitated waves that start
their boisterous candor underneath the ocean,
laughter is swift assertion of the heart.

Then comes a day to calibrate the shadows
knowing that dark can overbalance light.
Snows on the heart are deeper than on meadows;
one tear can drown the rains that drench the night.
And sadness whispers, like a silent chime,
through polyhedral attitudes of time.

NOW THE NORTH WIND

Along the sorrel valleys of September
the stormy breath of winter's basilisk
slants from the north and turns the earth to umber;
and blows a shadow on the milky disc
of sunlight, that is now a transitory
refracted ray caught in the undertow
of winter currents, like a secret story
sealed underneath the heart's high drifts of snow.

The voice of fear is sound of north wind sweeping
across the brooding meadows of the mind:
poignant and lonely as the muted weeping
of arid grasses; restlessly confined
beneath the camouflage of autumn art.
Fear, like cold winter rain, drips down the heart.

DISTANT DRUMMER

Hearing the multifarious wind express
an angry attitude, we pause to wonder
what demon-rages, what uncurbed duress,
provoke this mutiny of wind and thunder
that storm the house until the rafters tremble.
And we, though well-accustomed to the rain,
feel suddenly those ancient fears assemble
as cataclysmic clouds burst under strain.

When tempests pass, and tranquilness of summer
is imminent — nights luminous with stars —
that wind still echoes like a distant drummer,
ruffling the edges of forgotten scars;
blowing our subtle candles while we sleep.
Give me your hand. The nights grow chill and deep.

LOVE POEM

Astronauts of snow tumble past
your hospital window on earth orbits.
They free-fall down the darkness
that engulfs our lonely home.

This moment —
this one concatenate moment —
performs the improbable trick
of brushing us at the same time:
linking you, in your antiseptic bed,
and me, awkwardly dragging the trash
to the curbstone.

I clutch this moment,
laced in the snows of love,
as I have felt your nearness
when the black of a starless night
is blinding, and power lines of light
are downed by storm.

ARTICULATE APRIL

Day slowly knits into April evening
and the dark sweater of night
slips over the last remnant
of winter chill. The mood is ardent:

Youth leaps forward into uncertainty;
age finds the season richer
with a bundle of memories:

Those articulate nights — always
rolling away, like rivers — remembered
when wind whiffles the curtain
at an open window;
and the white dogwood tree
is a fall of moonlight on the mind . . .

Remembered when sounds obtrude upon sleep,
like the bang of a car door
and the buzz of a balky engine starting . . .
Or young laughter beneath our window
interlaced with the breath of hyacinths.

This poem for you
in wordless eloquence of April
when memories ripple,
like a piano medley,
on fluent fingers of a breeze.

ZERO HOUR

The voice of wind is suddenly still.
Winter's castanets that click
in restless fingers of every bough
are silent now.
This is the temporal pause
when over expectant air a chill
shatters the calm. Tides hang slack.
This is the moment when watches tick
louder than cannon. Hunger gnaws.
This is the second before applause
after a musician plays;
or the first chords of the wedding tune.

Spring is astir in a dark cocoon.
The chrysalis-tower
throbs and sways.
It should break within the hour.
Spring, incipient, feverishly
waits for the annual alchemy.

MOORINGS

Even with half-closed eyes before sleep falls
we see and hear the surf. Our minds, together,
drift shoreward to a town where salt wind calls
and waves, like children, tumble on each other.
A part of us is there. Although our home
is inland now, and circumscribed by trees,
the snow to us is always feathery foam;
and all the winds are sea-antiphonies.

Youth knits into the future. Take my hand
as, older now, we ravel to the past;
the way the waves roll up the hem of sand
then wear away the edges. Now, at last,
the mind assembles what the sight has lost.
And love is durable — wind-blown, wave-tossed.

FIREFLIES

Step softly, stranger, where toy comets spin
their luminous parabolas of light,
in blends of phosphorous and tourmaline,
along the ebon jungles of the night.
Move gently, as this meteoric band
of mini-stars among the underbrush
illuminates the dark. No leaf is fanned
by air or wing. The sultry summer hush
is broken by sonorous bull-frog choirs
from swamp-cathedrals, while this torch parade
ignites a thousand immemorial fires,
as though a thousand matches flashed and swayed.
A cricket starts his rusty metronome
and clocks intrepid fireflies winging home.

SOUND OF SEA

If you have heard the sound of sea you will hear it forever.
The sea will pattern your sleep when the loud day closes.
Eavesdropping stars will spy on the night and listen . . .
As the endless breaking of sea-waves superimposes.

If you have heard the sound of sea it will haunt you forever.
Always a wave will swell and then rise and climb
to incredible height, then crash . . . in a way that resembles
the shattering waters of time.

FROM CHANGELESS SHORE

AND

MOMENT IN TIME

CHANGELESS SHORE

Nothing will ever change beside this river:
there will be reeds bending, the water whisper,
forgotten oars tossed

where tides brush alluvial grasses,
a dinghy, ancient in sunlight,
fast to a broken wharf.

Loneliness, heavy as smoke,
will fall from wings of a heron;
a fish will shatter copper solitude

in a swift, reliable arc.
Nothing will ever be different here, no never.
Except freight of dead leaves on a dark tide:

the solemn removal of withered September,
nothing progresses, not even time.
We shall return to this place where silence whittles

shavings of time, drops them over the shore.
We shall return when blunt shadows fall.
We shall come back in the mind's long evening.

TOMBSTONES OF TIME

We heard the sibilance of waves
confiding to the sand and valedictory
of wind: an omen of endings.

Then, sudden as impromptu death,
a gray house by a gray sea
slipped away into gray shadow.

Only memory is substantial
in a world of abstractions.
We remember the summer of childhood,

when clatter of dishes in a reliable kitchen
sounded reveille: and woman-talk
on china-teacup afternoons, secretly

monitored by adolescents.
Lost youth is coeval with the stars.
Love now is *caveat emptor.* Faces

linger in doorways and then move on,
the way itinerant breakers rendezvous
with beaches and roll to other shores.

We are left with a handful of shadows
and a few chipped pieces of Limoges:
the tombstones of time.

REMEMBERED AUTUMN

Not a swift veering of wind to the north
but a sharp nostalgia signals the autumn.
For autumn is a remembered season:

September leaning its weight against August
and the essence of summer drained from the landscape
slowly, as blood chills in the veins, and wood-smoke

links chimney-by-chimney the souls of the houses.
Introspection creeps in with the mouse, uninvited;
and the mind forms a photograph in technicolor:

of red sweaters, of turquoise sky, of amber meadows,
and always children crossing streets,
and the sun's indecision.

Reprint the picture in the dark-room of winter
where pressed leaves are brittle as crackers,
and fingers of wind are a thief at the window.

For autumn is a season of memory,
falling two parts on the heart
and one part on the world.

SUMMER MORNING: NEW YORK

Trapezoids of sun press between buildings
and spread yellow blankets of heat
on city pavements.

Behind dim windows, where vapors
of fevered night stick to the eyes,
a thousand cups of coffee
attack barbiturate hangovers.
Only the sun never loses a night's sleep.

Secretaries, in a dead-heat with time,
pour from cliff-dwellings
into the leafless canyons.
Drama of day is shifting gears.

Jammed into crowded subways,
fears and frustrations brush shoulders
in an urban shuffle . . .
but never change places.
Sorrow is involute.

Morning newspapers conceal
the faces behind them
and screen the universal
from the private wars.

WINTER SONG

In after-wisdom, by winter firelight,
when shadows rise like braille
in a season of intimate rooms,
ambiguous lamps . . .
these verses written on snow.

Snow was deep upon the heart
that year; icicles, prison bars;
summer, a legend long forgotten.
Low sound of log-fire
balanced insufficient hours,
like a clock's escapement,
and accompanied your voice
with appropriate music.

Now on late evenings,
when winter is a wall around us;
and days, closed windows
in long panels of night,
there is only this ghostly fire,
an obbligato stripped of aria.

Heavy snow draws white blinds,
awaits the decision of winter.
Old wind leans
upon the crutch of time.
Soft on articulate tongues of flame
your voice returns in storied shadows . . .
These verses written on snow.

WOMEN ALONE

These lines for lonely women
in the unfamiliar rooms;
who speak a name in the night
and hear no answer;
who wait for the letter that never arrives;
wait and watch . . .
wait and watch . . .
in the shadow of sleep.

Words are the whisper-sound
of water falling, or a sigh of wind
in taffeta leaves, unheard
above whistles of trains not taken;
unheard above the mechanical street
that moves, conveyor-wise,
past shaded windows.

In dim light of the misty season,
when angers of youth fade to acceptance
and wisdom is wealth no longer solicited,
the lonely ones finger memories
like colored beads on a long chain of years;
and wait and watch . . .
wait and watch . . .
in the narthex of night.

So it is in towns and cities:
women in legions — unmobilized —
impotent in their aloneness,

searching for a handful of hope
in empty pockets of hours.

So it is in the mind's winter
when they wear the undergarment of silence
and wait in the dark that overlaps the day;
wait and watch . . .
wait and watch . . .
in the loges of time.

DEATH OF A HOUSE

Let it be written in darkness
that the family home is dead: killed
in conversion to a parking lot
by the wrecking ball of progress.
Fumes of commerce pollute
the burial place.

Dramas are frozen in flash-back;
childhood, static in tableau;
the voltage lost. The play-yard
is gone. But, held in long fingers
of the willow tree, a small girl
balances forever on the teeter-board
of time. Memory is a cripple
in the wheel-chair of the heart.

It was a seashore house;
salt wind in the rafters, and always
the hum of the wave's motor
as they vacuumed the sand.
On gray days mist rolled shoreward
like subliminal shadow —
as though the end were predestined.

One night the roofless staircase
ascended the interstellar highways
of the sky. And the Big Dipper
scooped out all the love.

EXODUS

Over northern trails roll station-wagon
caravans: those modern Conestogas
which are passports to suburbia.

Leaving the Deisel day
to irreconcilable cities,
people trade compressed houses
under a patchwork quilt of roofs
for the duplex — rancher — split level:
the mortgaged tickets to Middle America
where feet rest upon tenements
and arms reach upward to the stars.

They exchange porches for patios,
and the biographical clothesline-wash
for a maze of dials and push-buttons.
Housewives, upon whom suburbia pivots,
still rise early to start machinery of morning
and are caught in the pace of rural culture:
non-stop to eternity. In early

dusk of autumn, when air is weighted
with musk of dead leaves
and the brass knob of the moon
opens the door of night, older women
recall lost friends; and store memories
like jars of colored jellies
for the winter of time.

THE FEET OF TIME

Always the sound of footsteps echoes here
like shadows walking tiptoe in the fern
and bracken of an unremembered year.

Continuously they pass and never return.
Always a mist, a formidable shroud,
obscures a shape the mind does not discern.

Daylight, controlled by rheostat of cloud,
is indecisive. Only youth may know
the fearlessness of footsteps growing loud.

Youth legislates an ageless world, although
across the heart the hazy pantomime
moves ineluctably. Those winds that blow

down darkening years are sounds that fall and climb
like tennis-sneakers on the feet of time.

BEACH IN AUTUMN

Cold autumn sands stretch out white-ribbed and bare.
Bleak desolation of the wind and sea
erased remembered footprints that were there,

and swept the ghosts of summer's entity
upon the tuneless waves that wear away
the years; as though time, strumming listlessly

upon the dry reed-grass, scoffed at this day.
Deserted shells pick up the monotone
and chant it till their spiralled walls decay.

Down to this barren beach we come alone,
and build our fires against the stinging sweep
of wind-lashed sand. We see old friendships blown

in powdered grains of dust. Swift combers creep
like playful, summer children at their fling,
whose laughter left lost music in the deep,

wide-circling eddies, like a hidden spring,
to echo in a song the conches sing.

MONODY
(For C. M. L.)

I listen
for the sound of your voice:
where the pause of darkness
falls, a shower of sleep
upon the world;
where long and lonely beaches
lean patient ear
to catch secrets of ocean;
and on crowded city streets
where I move, thimble-size,
along arteries of intercourse.

But I hear only:
requiem of wind;
low dirge of waves;
and tin horns of industry . . .
which I cannot interpret!

In lexicons of stars
I seek your wisdom;
in banner of sunset;
in fine, lead pencil-script of rain.

But what do I find?
A match-point in the dark;
a ribbon for the evening;
ammunition of lost tears . . .
which I cannot interpret!

Once I almost felt you
in white dignity of snow.
But the touch was cold;
it was not yours.

Under the wide vault of sky
I wait,
where years march backward
in an echelon of nights.
I wait
in granite light of morning,
on empty doorsteps,
where days go by
like trains that never stop.
I wait
with hope, like tiny silver bells,
upon my heart . . .

REMEMBER THIS MAN

We speak for the man who walks alone,
who leans hard against the wind
and reads the cold commitments of stars.

He has no union, no lobby, no brotherhood . . .
no voice among the dissidents, the anarchists,
the militant marchers for power.

We speak for his silent legions
whose taxes turn the dynamos of government
and who hold the compass of conscience

clenched in the hand; and for the craftsman
who works all week for a Cadillac Sunday.
Remember this man. His creed

is inviolable as the ancient contract
between the moon and tides.
Justice hides behind the courthouse

and the dark is inimical to sleep.
Signs of protest are hyphens
compounding the cities. The hour is late . . .

We shadow-box with time.

BACK GATEWAYS

The approach to cities is through back gateways:
past a fretwork of steel tracks and dusty
boxcars with inventive names:
Seaboard, Lackawanna, Santa Fe
(the transient hide-outs of hoboes);

past mills and factories, and sooty houses
with postage-stamp yards that border
trenches of streets in continuous brick walls.
Somewhere a shabby child on a marble stoop
is stroking an alley cat.

Here, in the selvedge of the city
where threads of commerce and living
intertwine, spring comes only in window-boxes
with red geraniums of hope. The pattern

never changes in the polyglot towns:
Problems are open-end like investments of time.
Frenetic wind blows in circles always seeking
escape. And fear is tangible on the corners

of night. In the fast-falling dusk of youth
a girl peers through a smoky window
as city lights dazzle the dark
and disinherit the stars.